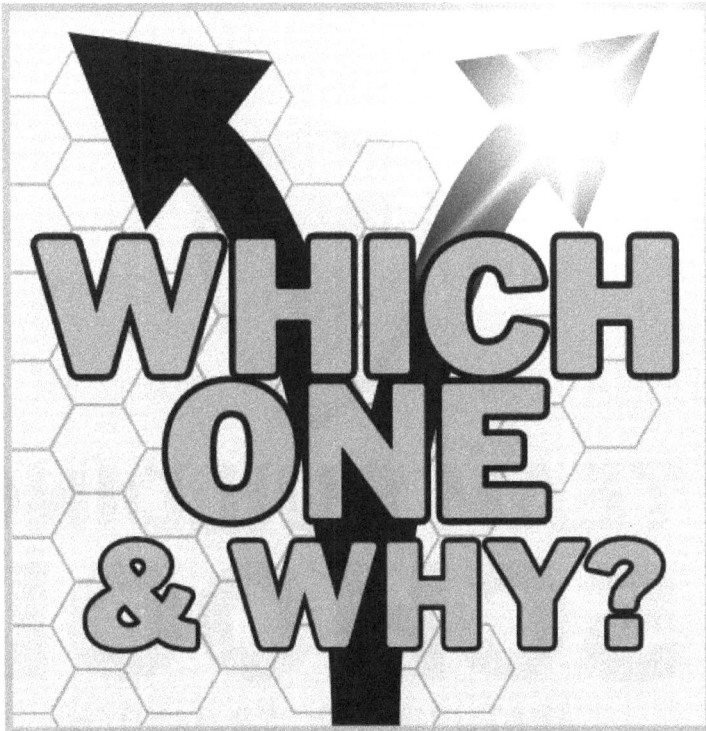

TEAM BUILDING
SCHOOL
FEATURING TYLER HAYDEN

Which One and Why? A Team Building Game

Published by Tyler Hayden,
Lunenburg, Nova Scotia
Canada

Cover: Tyler Hayden
Illustrations & Page Design: Steven Lacey
Distributed by Kindle Direct Publishing

Notional Library of Canada Cataloguing in Publication Hayden, Tyler, 1974-
Which One and Why?: A Team Building Game / Tyler Hayden.

E Book ISBN 978-1-897050-71-2
Print Book ISBN 978-1-897050-70-5

Business. 2. Education. 3. Games. I. Title.

Discover More Fun @ www.teambuildingschool.com

Which One and Why?
By Tyler Hayden

Warning - Use at Your Own Risk

FIND THIS FOR FREE ... WANT TO GIVE US A HIGH FIVE TO SAY THANK YOU?

We'd love you to BUY US A COFFEE or four - we like coffee. Head over to **www.teambuildingschool.com** and purchase your copy today.

TEAM BUILDING
SCHOOL
FEATURING TYLER HAYDEN

How to Play ...

Which One and Why? By Tyler Hayden

This game takes about 10 to 25 minutes to play. It is an entertaining and fun icebreaker/break-time activity that is inclusive. The educational intention is to encourage creative thinking in a fun and interactive way while encouraging communication and dialogue. Check out our full line of tools and activities at **www.teambuildingschool.com**.

Remember, the priorities are to have fun and play safe.

How to play:

1. The object of "Which One and Why?" is to complete one (or more) turns per person in your team. Based on your time limitations you choose the number of turns you can allot per person.

2. Assign one person to be in charge of a stopwatch or timer for the team. They will start and stop the timer accounting for the players 30 second (or so) response per question.

3. The person who has the biggest/heaviest pet gets to go first. This person reads the question aloud that is on the card to the team. For example, "Which one and Why – Be stuck in the elevator with your mother or mother-in-law?" This person will read the two choices. Then state their choice and give a brief reason as to why they chose that option. (Alternative: Team can vote on what they think readers' choice will be, prior to them presenting. Great with developed teams.)

4. After the team member has completed their turn, the card deck (book) is passed in a clock wise direction to the next team member. This continues until everyone has had a turn (or two).

TEAM BUILDING SCHOOL
FEATURING TYLER HAYDEN

Discover More Fun @ www.teambuildingschool.com

WHICH ONE & WHY?

Which would you choose?

Be stuck in the elevator with your,

A) Mother

B) Mother-in-Law.

TEAM BUILDING
SCHOOL
FEATURING TYLER HAYDEN

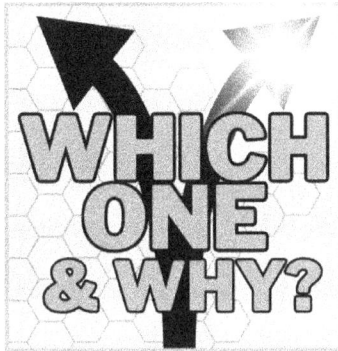

Which would you choose?

A) Travel in the Alps.

B) Travel in the Caribbean.

TEAM BUILDING
SCHOOL

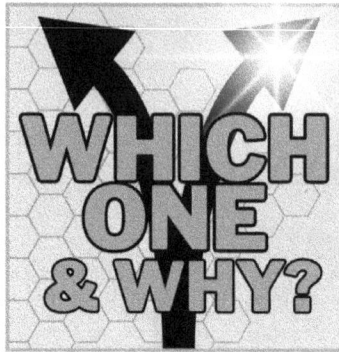
WHICH ONE & WHY?

Which would you choose?

A) Have a picnic at a landfill with your favourite star.

B) Dinner at the Four Seasons with your first boss.

Which would you choose?

A) Write a book that changes the life of one person I care about.

B) Write a bestselling trashy romance novel and strike it rich.

TEAM BUILDING
SCHOOL
FEATURING TYLER HAYDEN

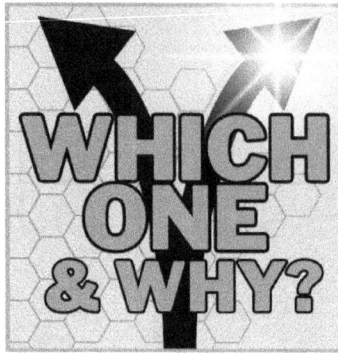

Which would you choose?

A) Be a farmer and live in a small town.

B) Be a taxi driver and live in the big city.

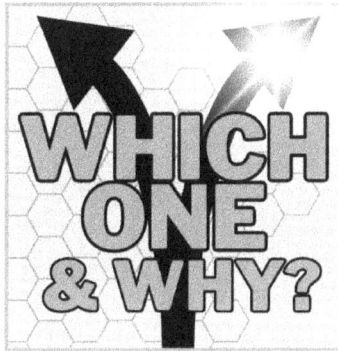

Which would you choose?

A) Own your own home that needs repairs.

B) Live in a condo that requires no maintenance.

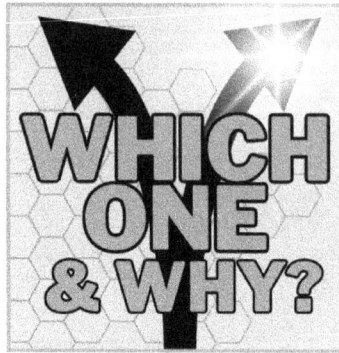

Which would you choose?

A) Sing for an AC/DC cover band.

B) Sing for a Spice Girls cover band.

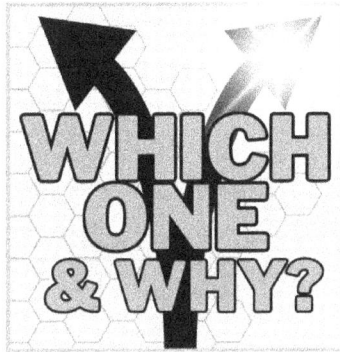

Which would you choose?

A) Paint a work of art.

B) Paint a room in a Habitat for Humanity home.

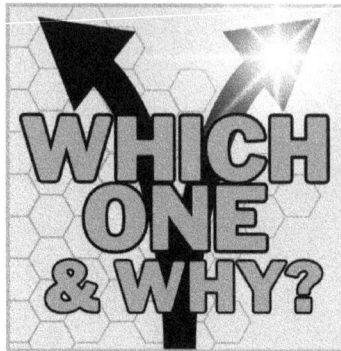

WHICH ONE & WHY?

Which would you choose?

A) Negotiate a peace deal between warring factions.

B) Negotiate a million-dollar commission business deal.

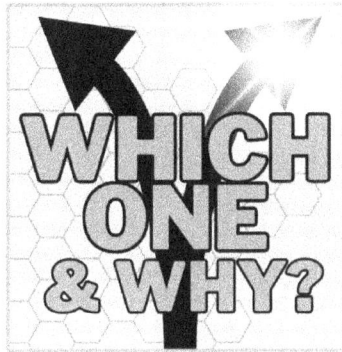

Which would you choose?

A) Dance in Public.

B) Dance in Private.

TEAM BUILDING
SCHOOL
FEATURING TYLER HAYDEN

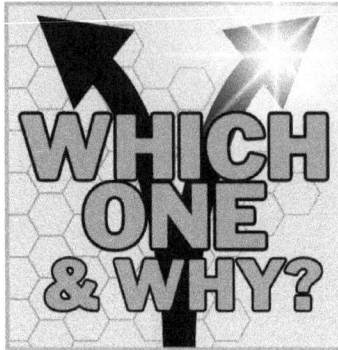

Which would you choose?

A) Be an Olympic Athlete.

B) Be a bestselling novelist.

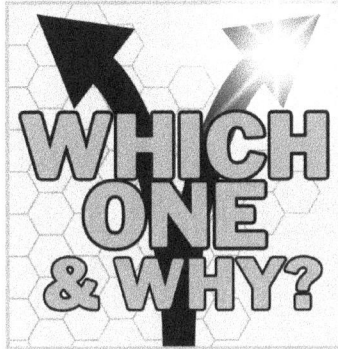

Which would you choose?

A) Live for a day as an Eagle.

B) Live for a day as a Great White Shark.

WHICH ONE & WHY?

Which would you choose?

A) Party late and "hoot with the owls."

B) Get up early and "scream with the eagles."

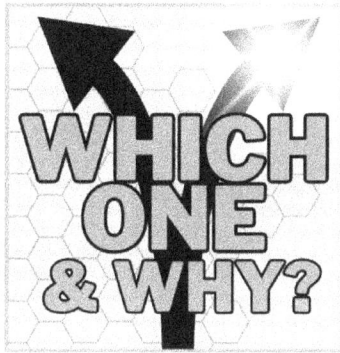

Which would you choose?

A) Die rich and hated.

B) Die poor and adored.

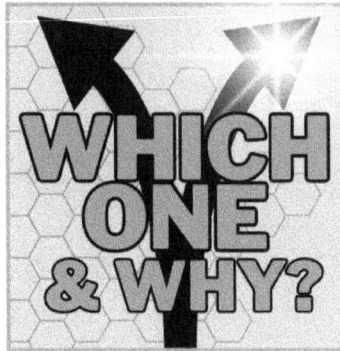

Which would you choose?

A) Open a trendy café.

B) Open a micro-brewery.

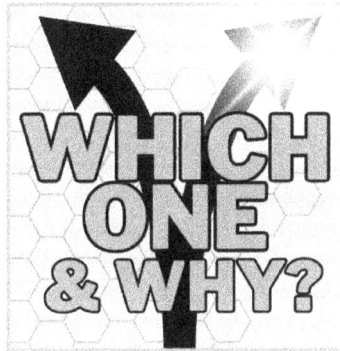

Which would you choose?

A) Be a teenager in the 1950's.

B) Be a teenager today.

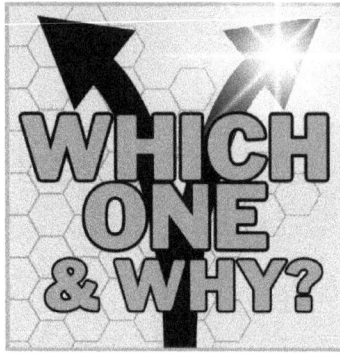

Which would you choose?

A) Invent a cure for cancer.

B) Invent the next "Google" sized digital innovation.

WHICH ONE & WHY?

Which would you choose?

A) Climb Mount Everest.

B) Go 20 000 leagues under the sea.

TEAM BUILDING
SCHOOL
FEATURING TYLER HAYDEN

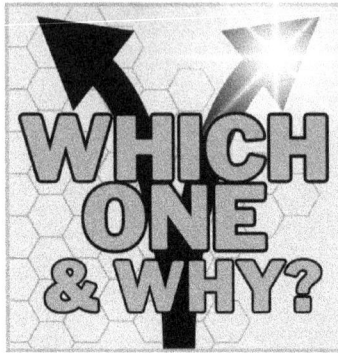

Which would you choose?

A) Be a storybook princess or prince.

B) Or the same books Villain or Villainess.

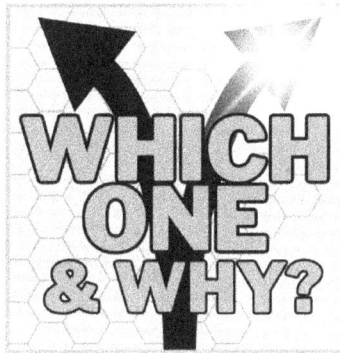

WHICH ONE & WHY?

Which would you choose?

A) Work in the woods as a Forest Ranger.

B) Work in the city as a member of the SWAT team.

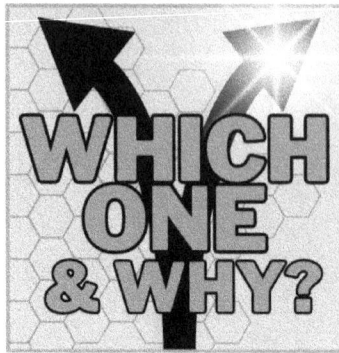

Which would you choose?

A) Retire and live by the beach.

B) Retire and live in the mountains.

TEAM BUILDING
SCHOOL
FEATURING TYLER HAYDEN

Which would you choose?

A) Work more and receive more money.

B) Work more and receive more vacation time.

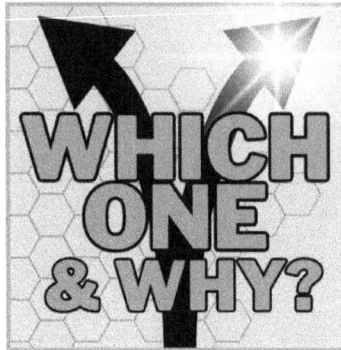

Which would you choose?

A) Clean up a crime scene.

B) Clean up an oil spill.

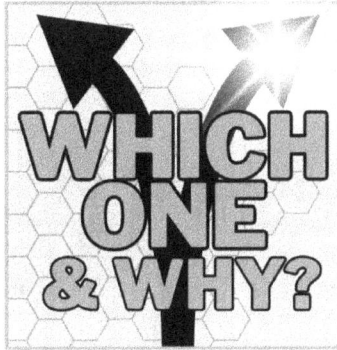

WHICH ONE & WHY?

Which would you choose?

A) Have three Cats.

B) Have three Dogs.

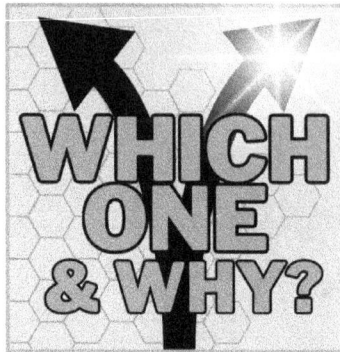
WHICH ONE & WHY?

Which would you choose?

A) Ride through the desert on a camel.

B) Ride through the foothills on horseback.

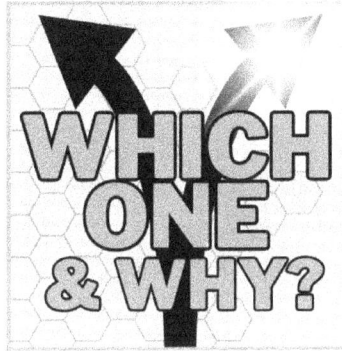

Which would you choose?

A) Drive a convertible sports car.

B) Drive a tricked-out motorcycle.

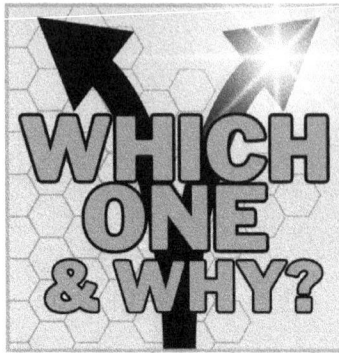

WHICH ONE & WHY?

Which would you choose?

A) Have someone tell you, you have bad breath.

B) Have them keep it to themselves.

TEAM BUILDING SCHOOL
FEATURING TYLER HAYDEN

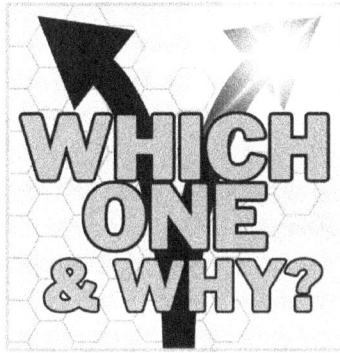

Which would you choose?

A) Direct a play on Broadway.

B) Be the star of the same play.

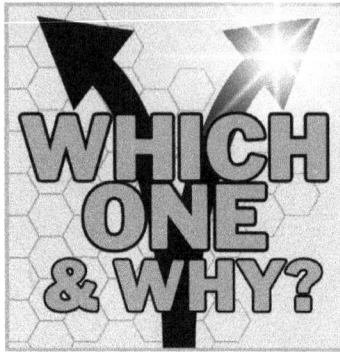

Which would you choose?

A) Be a megastar for one year.

B) Or hero/heroine in the eyes of your children forever.

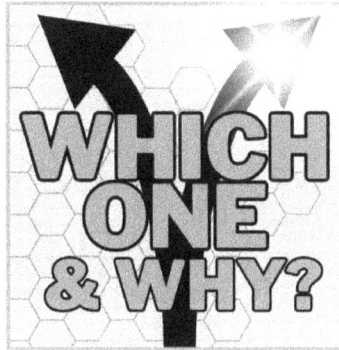

WHICH ONE & WHY?

Which would you choose?

A) Be the inventor of nuclear fusion.

B) Be the inventor of the internet.

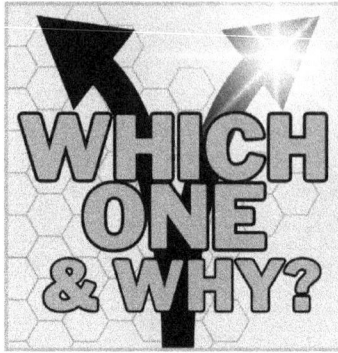

Which would you choose?

A) Be a Police Officer.

B) Be a Firefighter.

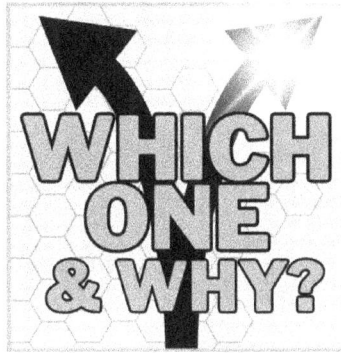

Which would you choose?

A) Participate in an Escape Room Challenge.

B) Participate in a Paint Night.

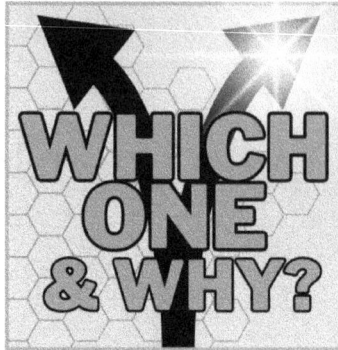

Which would you choose?

A) Win a free all expenses paid trip to Africa.

B) Win a brand-new luxury car.

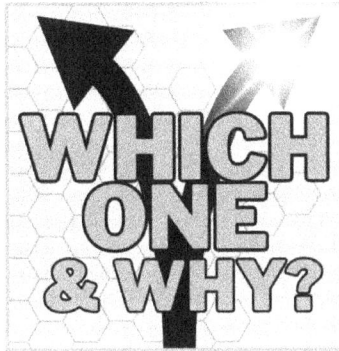

Which would you choose?

A) Pay off your mortgage.

B) Pay for your kids to get a post-secondary education.

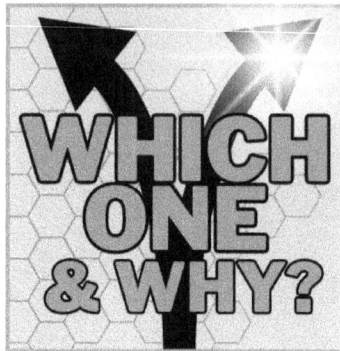

WHICH ONE & WHY?

Which would you choose?

A) Drive the fancy car you can't afford.

B) Drive the old Junker you can afford.

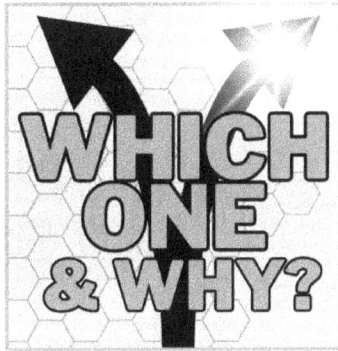

Which would you choose?

A) Take a loan to pay for a winter vacation to the beach.

B) Save money for two years and go debt free to the beach.

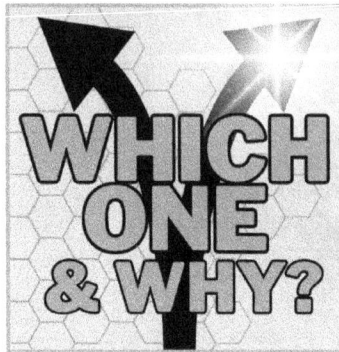

Which would you choose?

A) Relive your prom night.

B) Relive your wedding night.

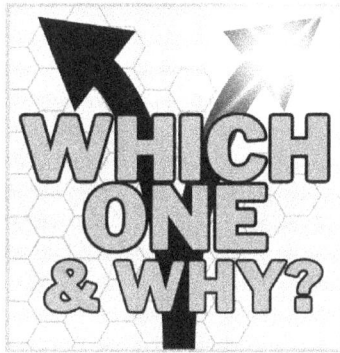

WHICH ONE & WHY?

Which would you choose?

A) Sit and chat with your best friend for an hour.

B) Meet someone new/ interesting and talk for an hour.

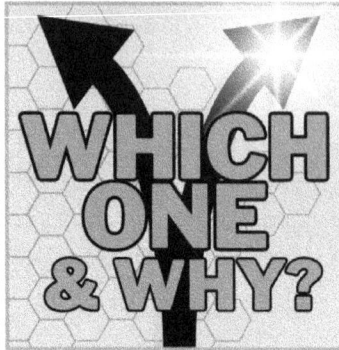
WHICH ONE & WHY?

Which would you choose?

A) Quickly pocket the $100 you find on the ground.

B) Look around and try to find the owner for that $100.

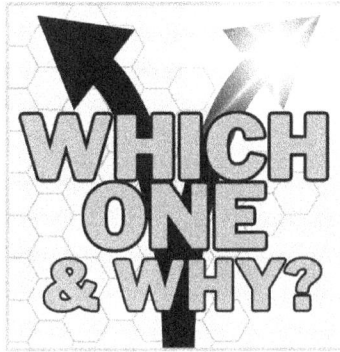
WHICH ONE & WHY?

Which would you choose?

A) Drive the speed limit on the highway.

B) Push the gas pedal down and speed down the highway.

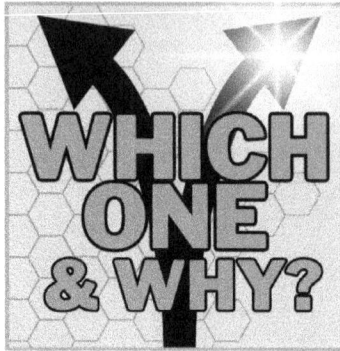

Which would you choose?

A) Ask for permission.

B) Ask for forgiveness.

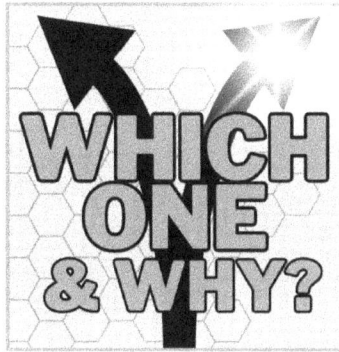

WHICH ONE & WHY?

Which would you choose?

A) Snack on a piece of fruit.

B) Snack on a chocolate bar.

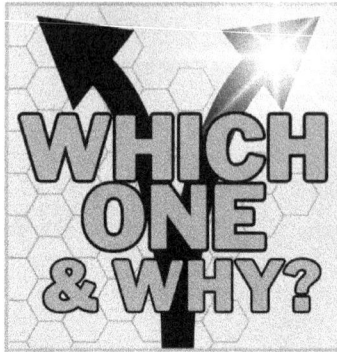

Which would you choose?

A) Have tea with the Queen.

B) Or Freddy Mercury of Queen.

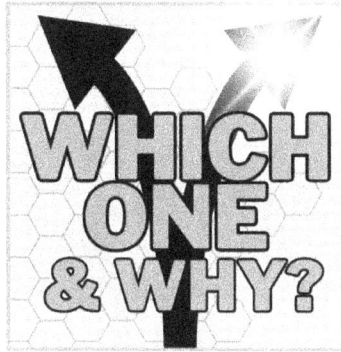

Which would you choose?

A) Be caught in a rain storm.

B) Be caught in a snow storm.

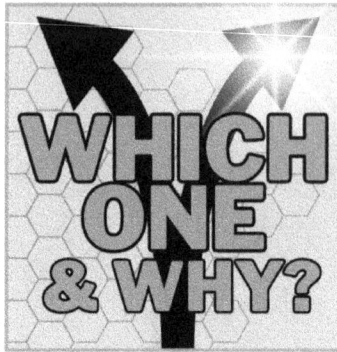
WHICH ONE & WHY?

Which would you choose?

A) "Toot" in a public place.

B) Hold it and feel the pain.

WHICH ONE & WHY?

Which would you choose?

A) Give great presents.

B) Receive great presents.

TEAM BUILDING
SCHOOL
FEATURING TYLER HAYDEN

WHICH ONE & WHY?

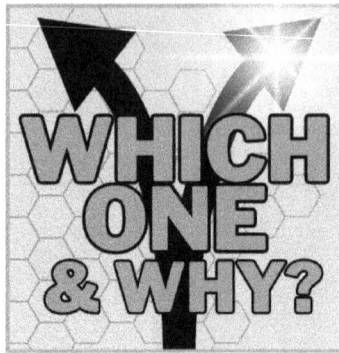

Which would you choose?

A) Eat your last supper with someone you always wanted to meet.

B) Or someone you love.

WHICH ONE & WHY?

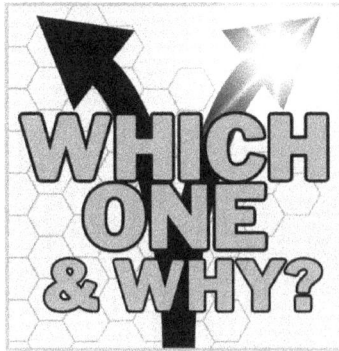

Which would you choose?

A) Go out dancing.

B) Stay home and watch a movie.

TEAM BUILDING
SCHOOL
FEATURING TYLER HAYDEN

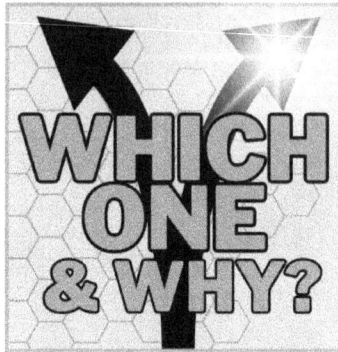

WHICH ONE & WHY?

Which would you choose?

A) Be known for your beauty.

B) Be known for your intelligence.

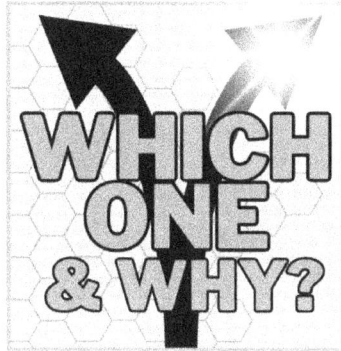

Which would you choose?

A) Save a dog.

B) Save a drug addict.

WHICH ONE & WHY?

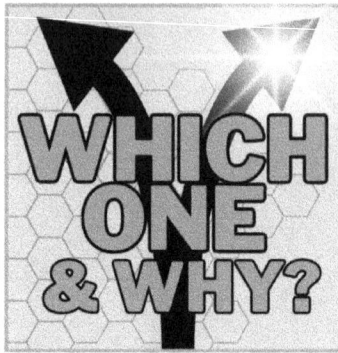

Which would you choose?

A) Wear nice jewelry.

B) Wear brand name clothing.

TEAM BUILDING
SCHOOL
FEATURING TYLER HAYDEN

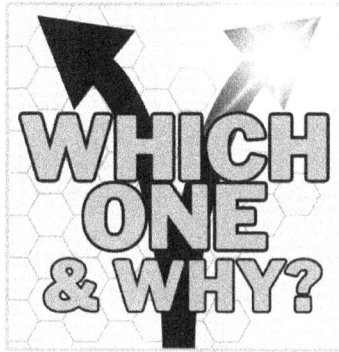

Which would you choose?

A) Be Darth Vader.

B) Be Luke Skywalker.

WHICH ONE & WHY?

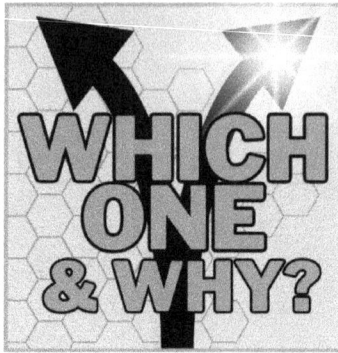

Which would you choose?

A) Go to an NBA Game.

B) Go to an NFL Game.

TEAM BUILDING
SCHOOL
FEATURING TYLER HAYDEN

WHICH ONE & WHY?

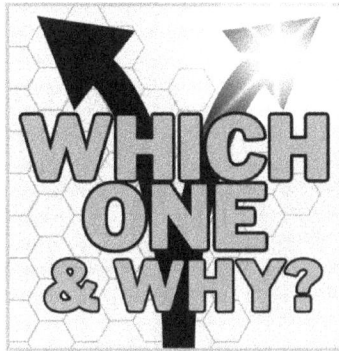

Which would you choose?

A) Swim with sharks.

B) Go Skydiving.

TEAM BUILDING
SCHOOL
FEATURING TYLER HAYDEN

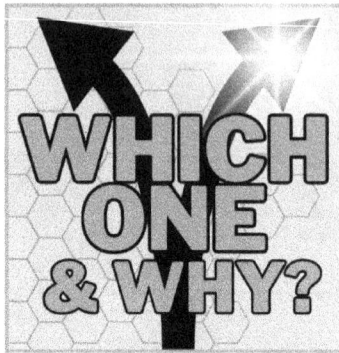

Which would you choose?

A) Prepare a fine meal.

B) Eat a fine meal.

WHICH ONE & WHY?

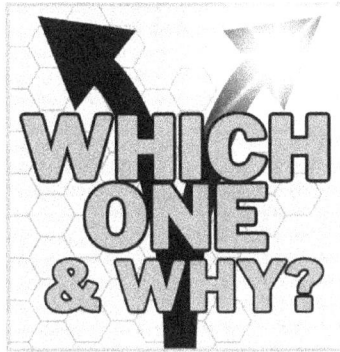

Which would you choose?

A) Be a Sumo Wrestler.

B) Be a MMA Fighter.

TEAM BUILDING
SCHOOL

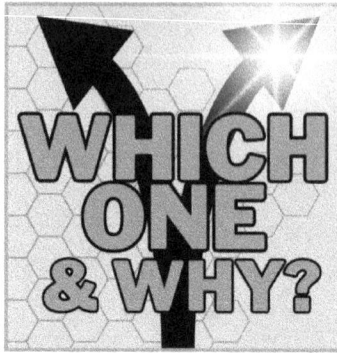
WHICH ONE & WHY?

Which would you choose?

A) Wear your parents clothes.

B) Wear your kids clothes.

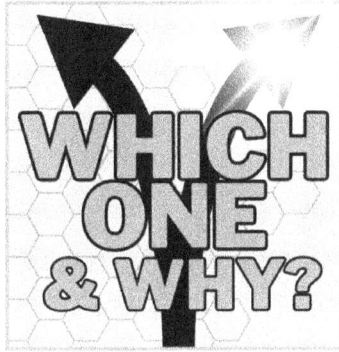

Which would you choose?

A) Apprentice with Donald Trump.

B) Apprentice with Robin Williams.

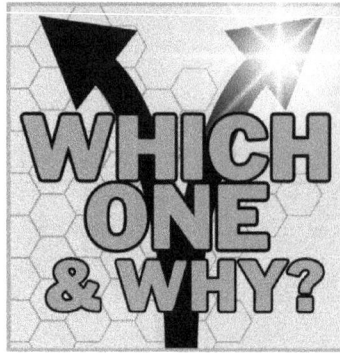

Which would you choose?

A) Live in an apartment with a housekeeper.

B) Live in a mansion alone.

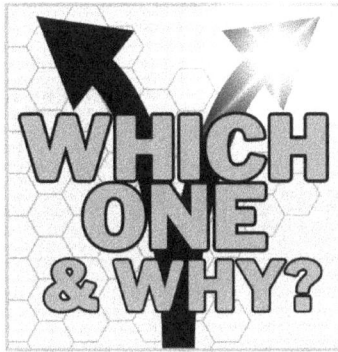

Which would you choose?

A) Be transformed into a cartoon Dora the Explorer.

B) Or Scooby Doo.

WHICH ONE & WHY?

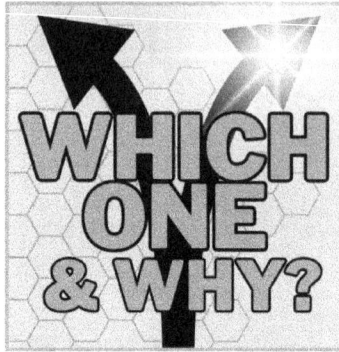

Which would you choose?

A) Renovate a dilapidated old home.

B) Or Buy a brand new one.

TEAM BUILDING
SCHOOL
FEATURING TYLER HAYDEN

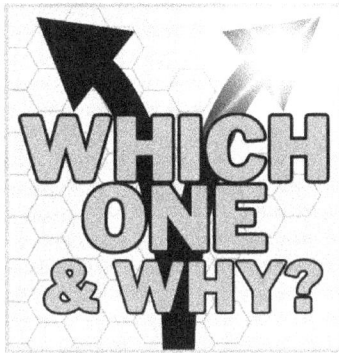

Which would you choose?

A) Visit the polar bears.

B) Visit the pyramids.

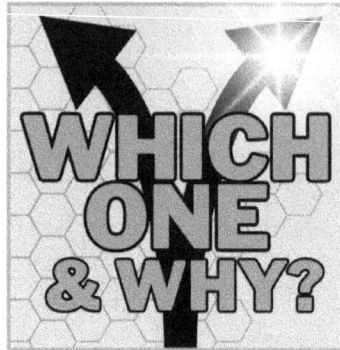

Which would you choose?

A) Adventure with Sir Richard Branson.

B) Or Oprah.

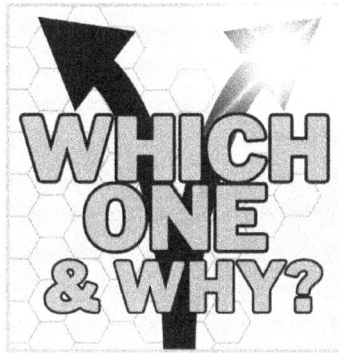

Which would you choose?

A) Own a profitable ethical stock.

B) Or uber profitable non-ethical stock.

WHICH ONE & WHY?

Which would you choose?

A) Be a children's film star.

B) Be a Soap Opera star.

TEAM BUILDING
SCHOOL
FEATURING TYLER HAYDEN

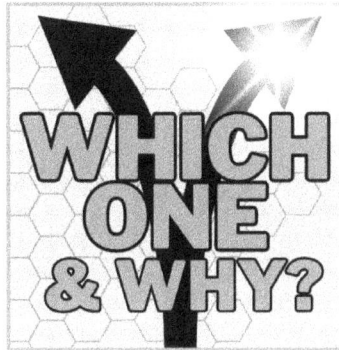

WHICH ONE & WHY?

Which would you choose?

A) Run for leader of the country and win.

B) Be the CEO of the country's largest company.

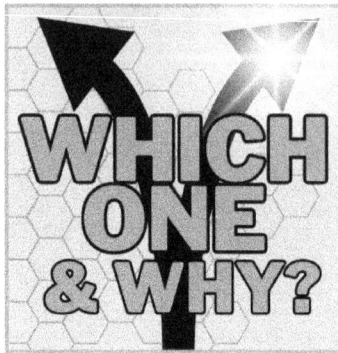

Which would you choose?

A) Redo Elementary School.

B) Redo High School.

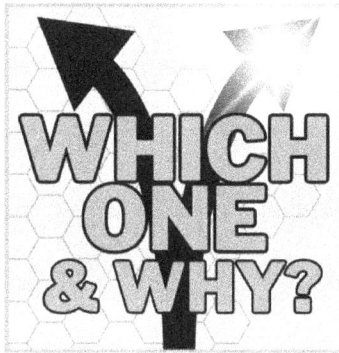

Which would you choose?

A) Spend the day with your grandparent.

B) Spend the day with your favourite teacher or coach.

WHICH ONE & WHY?

Which would you choose?

A) Be a doctor at an emergency scene.

B) Be an onlooker.

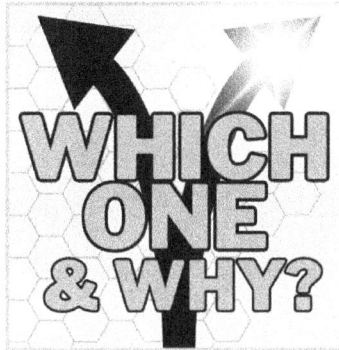

Which would you choose?

A) Play professional hockey.

B) Play professional golf.

WHICH ONE & WHY?

Which would you choose?

A) Be on a reality TV show.

B) Watch your best friend win a reality TV Show.

TEAM BUILDING
SCHOOL

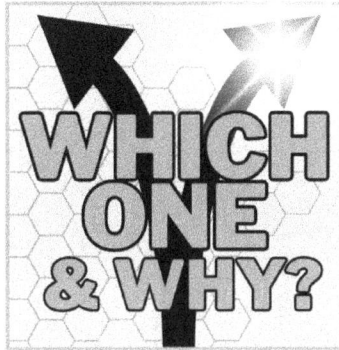

Which would you choose?

A) Be the main character of a spy movie.

B) Be the main character of a horror flick.

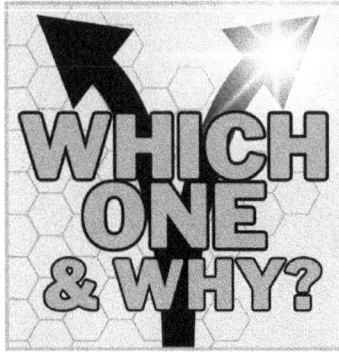

Which would you choose?

A) Open an Art Gallery.

B) Open a Toy Store.

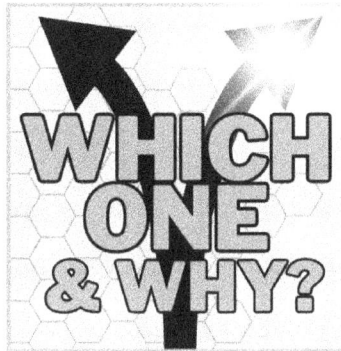
WHICH ONE & WHY?

Which would you choose?

A) Go on a night out to a live theatre presentation.

B) Go on a night out to a Rock music concert.

TEAM BUILDING
SCHOOL
FEATURING TYLER HAYDEN

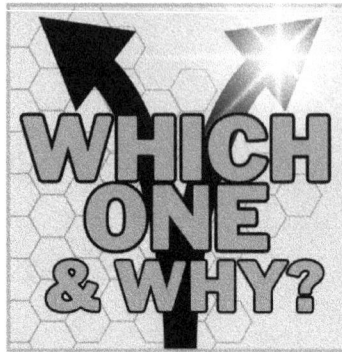
WHICH ONE & WHY?

Which would you choose?

A) Go on a road trip with your Mother/Father-in-law.

B) Go on a road trip with your mother and father.

TEAM BUILDING
SCHOOL
FEATURING TYLER HAYDEN

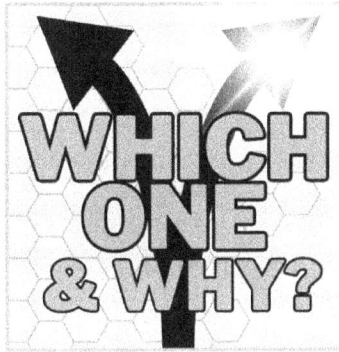

Which would you choose?

A) Eat take out.

B) Eat a home cooked meal.

TEAM BUILDING
SCHOOL

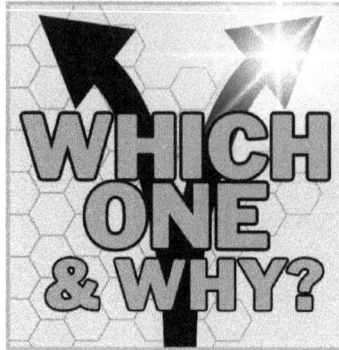

Which would you choose?

A) Kill the big furry spider.

B) Capture the big furry spider and take it outside.

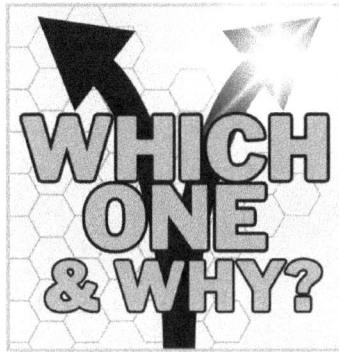

WHICH ONE & WHY?

Which would you choose?

A) Be a scientific scholar.

B) Be an evangelist.

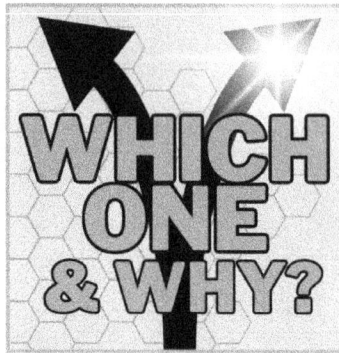

Which would you choose?

A) Live by the letter of the law.

B) Live in the grey area of the law.

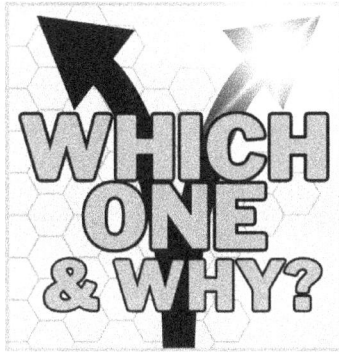
WHICH ONE & WHY?

Which would you choose?

A) Host a family reunion.

B) Host a high school grad class reunion.

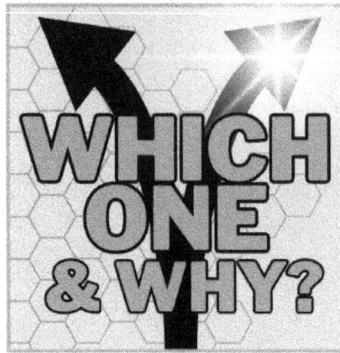

Which would you choose?

A) Live in your country of residence.

B) Live in another country.

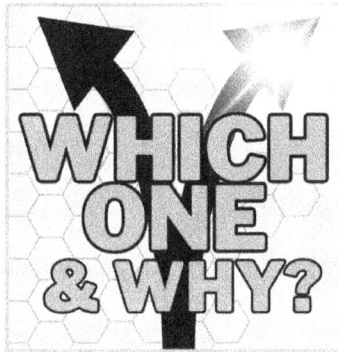

WHICH ONE & WHY?

Which would you choose?

A) Drive a Harley Davidson.

B) Drive a VW Van.

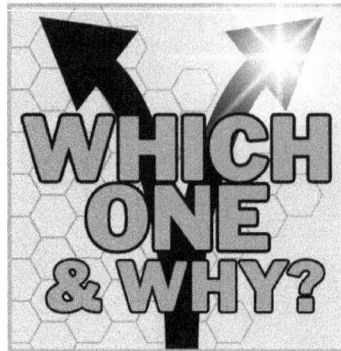

Which would you choose?

A) Fast forward and live in the next century.

B) Rewind and live in the last century.

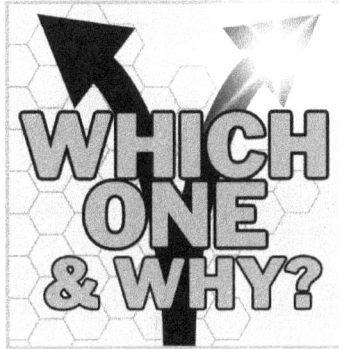

Which would you choose?

A) Eat table scraps from a fancy restaurant.

B) Eat fast-food.

TEAM BUILDING
SCHOOL
FEATURING TYLER HAYDEN

WHICH ONE & WHY?

Which would you choose?

A) Play a round of golf
   with Tiger Woods.

B) Play a round of golf
   with Adam Sandler.

TEAM BUILDING SCHOOL
FEATURING TYLER HAYDEN

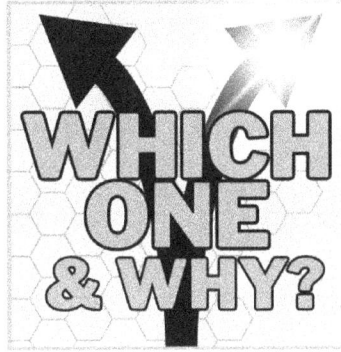

Which would you choose?

A) Go on a road trip across the country.

B) Go on a transatlantic ocean voyage.

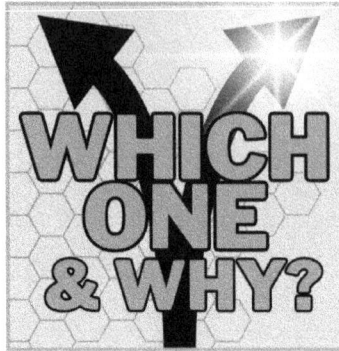

Which would you choose?

A) Have a campfire beside the beach with friends.

B) Go on a date to the park and listen to a string quartet.

TEAM BUILDING
SCHOOL
FEATURING TYLER HAYDEN

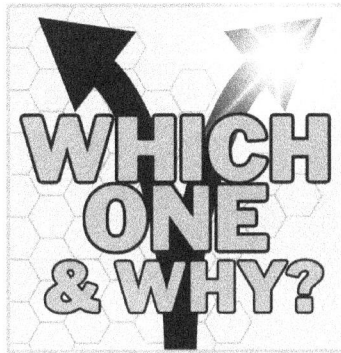
WHICH ONE & WHY?

Which would you choose?

A) Spend a night in a haunted house.

B) Spend a night in a motel room beside a busy highway.

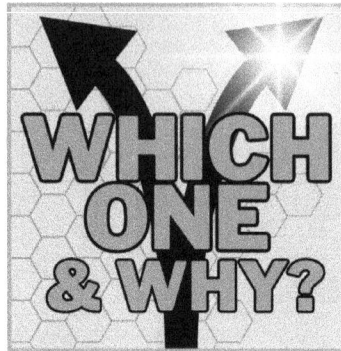

Which would you choose?

A) Take a ride on a roller coaster.

B) Take a ride on a carousel.

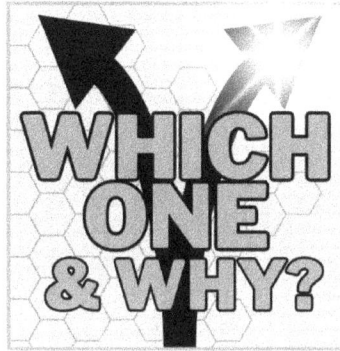

Which would you choose?

A) Give **$100 000** to an environmental charity.

B) Give **$100 000** to a homeless initiative.

TEAM BUILDING
SCHOOL
FEATURING TYLER HAYDEN

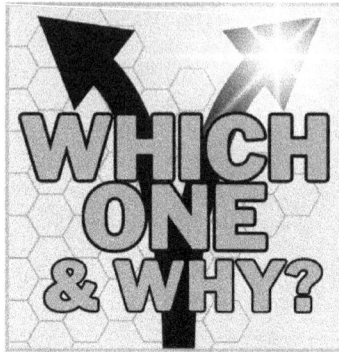

WHICH ONE & WHY?

Which would you choose?

A) Be an social media influencer.

B) Be a local community change agent.

TEAM BUILDING
SCHOOL
FEATURING TYLER HAYDEN

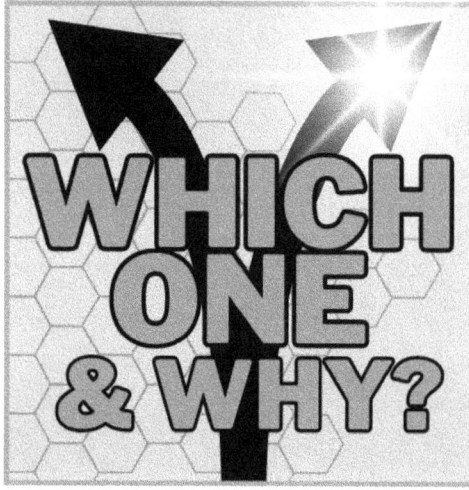

WHICH ONE & WHY?

Thank You for Playing with Us.

TEAM BUILDING SCHOOL

FEATURING TYLER HAYDEN

Download amazing Team Building
Tools & Take Certificate Courses at:

www.teambuildingschool.com

**Learn More & book Tyler for your next
Keynote or Team Event:**

www.tylerhayden.com

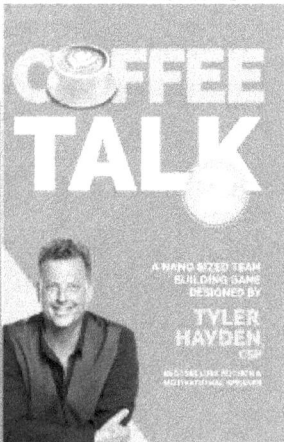

**Find more
great books and activities at:**

www.tylerhayden.com/shop

Who is this Guy?

Tyler Hayden CSP, is a keynote speaker like you've never experienced before!

Since 1996, Tyler continues to be a sought after internationally respected team building designer, best-selling author, and business speaker. He delivers a powerful punch that inspires teams, innovates management techniques, and invigorates team engagement.

When it comes to empowering audiences and teams to succeed—and to be their best every day—Tyler leads the way with insight and laughter.

His team building workshops and motivational keynote speeches receive rave reviews from managers and business leaders alike. "Energizing," "hilarious," "who knew learning could be this much fun." and "ideas I can easily implement," are things regularly said by Tyler's clients about his keynotes and team building events.

He is the author of over twenty-five books and the creative mind behind 100s of powerful and fun team building products including: Virtually Engaged Team Building Activities, The Business that Cared About People, The 14-Minute Mentor, Livin' Life Large, Father's & Mother's Message in a. Bottle, TEAM Activities, and More.

Tyler is a thought leader who works internationally with Fortune 500, Inc 5000 and Premier Associations to level-up their learning design. Tyler's innovative gamification and in-depth understanding of multiple intelligences yields programs that increase engagement and learning in amazingly simple ways.

Some of his past clients include: Subway, Michelin, Honeywell, YPO, Subaru, TD Bank, Pratt & Whiteny, and more.

Make sure your seat backs are up and your table trays are stowed, because we are about to unleash Canada's Answer to Alternative Energy ...

Invite Tyler to Speak at your Next Event
www.tylerhayden.com

🚀 Scan to Learn More 🚀

TEAM BUILDING
SCHOOL
FEATURING TYLER HAYDEN

www.ingramcontent.com/pod-product-compliance
Lightning Source LLC
Chambersburg PA
CBHW071516200326
41519CB00019B/5960